CAT TALES:
DA REAL PUSSY

CAT TALES:
DA REAL PUSSY

MICK E. JONES

Library of Congress Control Number:		2013903483
ISBN:	Hardcover	978-1-4836-0056-7
	Softcover	978-1-4836-0055-0
	Ebook	978-1-4836-0057-4

This book was printed in the United States of America.

Rev. date: 06/02/2014

To order additional copies of this book, contact:
Xlibris LLC
1-888-795-4274
www.Xlibris.com
Orders@Xlibris.com
598020

TABLE OF CONTENTS

DEDICATION

Dedication pages are usually written to pay tribute and express appreciation for those people who have assisted, supported, inspired, and encouraged the author to successfully achieve his or her personal writing goal.

For me, the greatest accolades belong to God, the Supreme Spirit. I truly believe, and have strong conviction that God is entirely responsible for the writing of *Cat Tales: Da Real Pussy*. I therefore, give high praise of thanks to you, Heavenly Father-Mother.

God, since I know, that your will is done through people, I do give thanks to you and to the people you have chosen to be the hedge around me, beginning with Mr. and Mrs. Wilbur D. Jones, my earthly mother and father, through whom you embodied and channeled me. I will always honor them in your name, that I may receive the promise of longer days on your planet Earth. Thank you!

I thank you Father God for womanhood, the sacred vessel through which you produced motherhood, my mother, and the wonderful sisters who loved, understood, and praised my writings. To the sisters Nia Terry, Lorretta Alston, Barbra Burke Tatum, Ayanna Terry, Rebecca "Tootsie" Allen, Little Wilma Little, Gwen Bridges, Gayle "Fish" Bonner, Lucy Scott, Janice "Mum" Melton, Susan Lambert, Halimah Brooks, and Josephine "Big Jo" Molten.

And of course, there is the brotherhood, the shroud and foundation of fatherhood, "2Da Hood." I sincerely thank the brothers who cared and shared their positive and constructive feedback to these writings: Darryl Dane Bohanan, "Da Big Head"; Gene "Jack-E Jack" Clark; Jerard Childs; Dr. Zuzillion; Chris Jennings; Ben Jerand; Joel McCray, "Uncle Joe"; Chris Birkett, and Edgar Weicks.

Finally, the Johnnies-come-lately. But! Better late than never. Amy Berkeley, Kenny Biter, Kathleen Elfallah, Nate "the Great" House, Clare Sullivan, and Peter "Da Rock" Jensen.

A hearty thanks to Toren Michael Jones, my darling son, the inheritor, by God's spirit, of the same humanity that produced *Cat Tales: Da Real Pussy*; the vessel God has chosen to give me the privilege and honor of passing on His torch of love. The father and son are one. I love you, so much!

Last, but never least or less, the *piece de résistance*, my dear darling precious wife, one flesh in union with God. The womb of man, a gift. I thank you for your patience to tolerate and persevere. It took a little longer than desired. But! Because of our faith, I was finally published. We kept the faith, and faith produces when it is unwavering and in one accord with doing the will of our Father. Thank you, my precious darling, Sue!

Peace y'all and congratulations.
Much love––God bless.

Mick E. Jones

CAT TALES
INTRODUCTION

Ahh! I'm feeling so refreshed, so relaxed, and so rejuvenated with my pen in hand. My dependable pen is an old friend that I can count on for consistency, faithfulness, and obedience. My pen and I are like family; we've been together through thick and thin.

When I'm inspired to pick up my dear friend the pen, something happens! Inspiration comes through clearly and distinctively during quiet, meditative talks with the spirit of God within.

After this rapture of loving communication, I become charged and spiritually exhilarated, and as it is referred to in religious parlors, I'm on fire and I'm full. I am transformed to transcribe.

It is a very reassuring fullness, this fulfilling feeling of "I have something to say" because my cup runneth over. This is when I pick up my friend the pen to let the flow begin. And as scriptures say, it's written.

It's all good, the spirit within, self-expression through my dear friend the pen, doing its thing. Write on, write on!

At this point in time, the pen has decided to translate my feelings and reflections on my experiences with cats. The following is the written version of *Cat Tales*, so let's get it on!

Why tales about cats? I have always been extremely intrigued by cats because of their unpredictable and bizarre behavior and their mystical quality.

I don't favor cats over dogs. For the record, I'm not pro cats or pro dogs. Cats are profound, and for the sake of my written expression, they are quite prolific in my opinion.

Cats have the depth of someone with a PhD, and experts of social behavior have equated their characteristics to women. Cats are a feminine symbol of womanhood. Common phrases include "Here pussy." It's funny how humans relate themselves to members of the animal kingdom. Me and my pen, we're relating to cats in the authentic *Cat Tales*.

And again for the record, I don't favor cats over dogs, blacks over whites, Jews over Christians, gays over heterosexuals, etc. I think you all get my open-penned point of view. I believe in the belief that if God's not a respecter of persons, why should I be? And I'm not pro cat.

It's just that cats have been messing with me and there's a lot to write about. My friend the pen and I want to share this *"cat-messing"*. So, sit back and enjoy the mess of tales about cats. It may just be the cat's meow, but it's definitely not the kitty litter.

We will open with Elmo, the stimulant response for the unfolding of our cat journey.

ELMO

Elmo is a very interesting neighborhood cat. Elmo is a slender, wiry, taut-built cat, strong and cunning. Elmo's basic coloring is dirty blond, with a slight orange tint to it. Elmo's face is white, and the whiteness continues down onto his underbody.

Elmo parades around our neighborhood like it was his own, almost patrolling it like a soldier. His owner, Dan, is a Vietnam veteran; maybe Elmo has been trained. Elmo is extremely skillful at waiting, watching, tracking, trapping, catching, and destroying field mice.

One time, Elmo caught a seagull. The seagull must have been disoriented, delirious, and very hungry or something. Or maybe the seagull got some crack at Venice Beach and now is tripping in Hollywood.

Anyway, the seagull landed in the yard in front of our apartment. And Elmo, in one of his camouflage modes, jumped out of the barbecue pit and took out Livingston the Seagull; so much for the classics.

Elmo is the top kick and has reconnaissance experience and tenure. Elmo's like Bruce Springsteen, and he's the boss. Elmo takes care of business and runs the neighborhood, taking names and throwing them down.

I remember when Elmo picked me out to get to know him and have a special relationship with him. Elmo didn't cozy up to everyone. Sometimes he would throw his tail up in the air and sashay around and wouldn't let anybody touch him, including his owner.

I recall hearing his owner saying, "Okay, be finicky, but remember, you ain't Morris the Cat. You ain't got no agent. Hell, you ain't even in the union. And if you are, they're on strike!"

I would always catch a glimpse of Elmo checking me out from various strategically located points of observation. In fact, he would study my whole family. He got so studious with us that he recognized our car.

Finally Elmo broke the ice one day. He brought me a robin redbreast and laid it in front of our door and placed it thoughtfully on our welcome doormat. I told him, "Thanks, Elmo, but no thanks. The only bird I eat is from the KFC, government inspected, you know!"

Elmo had become a personal item with the family. He would run up to us, purr, and rub against us. Elmo would get his daily strokes and pats, get a paw-five, and stroll off.

Then there were times when none of us were even allowed to touch Elmo. He said "no way" with his body language.

I first met Elmo when I was parking my car and Elmo jumped up on top of the hood and strolled up to look at me, peering through the windshield while pushing his face up against the glass.

I sat there watching him staring into my eyes. His bluish-green eyes moved back and forth intensely and placidly, yet with compassion. Elmo's eyes were soft and gentle in their expression, as if Elmo was trying to express how much he liked me, or at least how much he respected me.

He had made his final decision based on time spent strategically observing me with my family, neighbors, and other animals. Elmo had witnessed me doing the neighborhood watch. He knew that I spent time beautifying the neighborhood, feeding, clothing, and giving to the poor, starving and hungry, both humans and animals. I gave everything from spare change to nuts and breadcrumbs; Elmo respected all this.

And to further demonstrate our closeness, Elmo would sit at my feet while his owner Dan and I swapped service stories.

Elmo was on the hood of my car, staring into my eyes, moving with the grace of a skilled acrobat. Elmo stepped onto the outside rearview mirror then walked along the window frame on the driver's side and stuck his head inside the window while balancing himself on three legs. His two hind legs were perched on the outside rearview mirror with his front left leg planted on the window frame. He had a little impish look in his eyes, and he playfully slapped me in the face with his right paw. And with the speed of the great cats, Elmo was down on the ground running.

He went running into our haven, a plush and well-landscaped, gated, fenced-in yard. It was a sculptured paradise garden with numerous jade bushes, cactuses, rosebushes, and trees. It was a place of much joy for a cat, or any animal for that matter.

As I watched Elmo scamper happily away, I laughed out loud and heartily yelled, "You gonna get yours, Elmo!"

The Elmo connection became a daily ritual, one that was very warm and affectionate. In fact, Elmo would be at the door when my wife Sue was leaving to teach at a nearby school and our sixteen-year-old son Toren was heading for school.

I took much pride and joy in watching my family leave for their respective places in life. I stayed put with my friend the pen to write.

When my family left, that's when the magic seemed to happen and Elmo began his *"Elmoisms"*. He usually was at the door meowing to get his morning rubs and then to go on his local neighborhood patrol. This had gotten fairly routine, and everybody seemed so enamored with this daily pattern that Elmo was becoming family. At least he acted like it. And his cat act was quite convincing. Elmo was a player, and cats certainly are great actors.

Elmo's friendly behavior toward the family was a play on life. Elmo was too cool for the room. It's funny how the relationship of the coolest of comrades can get cold.

And this frigid condition would soon become the climatic barometer of a chilly atmospheric degree. An attitude that would create the storm cloud that would hover over our relationship with Elmo. A forecast clash can expect some light precipitation. This light precipitation would begin to fall when Rocky fell to earth.

Rocky was a very self-confident and gregarious, unusual character. Rocky's presence and good intentions were well meaning, but as it has been quoted, "The way to hell is paved with good intentions."

Rocky would threaten paradise and put an end to unity in the community. Rocky was a flying squirrel, a heart and scene stealer. He was now on the stage with Elmo, a player in his own right and no second banana.

Don't ask me how these things happen or why they happen to me; they just do. I used to think it was a curse. Now I know it's a blessing, a gift from God, just the life course that I'm on, a natural healing. It's real and I'm Dr. Feel Good.

If I'm not a doctor, then I sure started to feel like Dr. Doolittle when I began talking to the animals. And they seemed to understand what I was talking about. In the blink of an eye, I had become Uncle Remus and Dr. Doolittle.

I would suddenly have an impulse to do a little feeding. I fed the birds dried rice, grain, and corn and put peanuts out for the squirrels. This is when Rocky would swoop to the ground.

Rocky had been observing me while he was perched on a limb in one of the numerous trees in the yard, but mostly from the tree directly in front of our apartment. On this particular day, Rocky swooped down and the story began.

Rocky was sitting in front of me, sitting up on his hind legs and twitching his nose, fluttering his eyes. Then he got down and ran past me, right up our stairs. He went right to the peanuts and ate one immediately. He took another one, ran off, and hid it under a bush. He came back, got another peanut, and buried it under the cactus. He did this numerous times. In the meantime, I had gotten more peanuts.

I sat on the top step and placed some peanuts close to me. When Rocky returned for more, he had to come closer to me. He approached the peanuts very casually and was secure with the conditions I had presented. He was all right with the peanuts being close to me; he got 'em anyway!

It was on the next gathering of the peanuts that the real breakthrough was revealed. I had placed all the peanuts on the top of my legs. My legs were extended down the staircase as I sat on the top of the stair landing.

Returning energetically as he left, Rocky came bounding up the stairs. Just as he hit the top step, I saw his eyes do a quick spot check; he didn't see any peanuts. Then his nose directed his focus to me. Rocky saw the peanuts on the top of my legs, between the knees. He casually sashayed and moseyed over and sniffed me, then jumped onto my leg, got a nut, and took off!

The real clincher or perfect indicator of how far and how intimate our relationship would become was the time Rocky came up the steps. As he was stepping onto the landing, I was back in the apartment in the doorway with the door open wide. I was lying on the floor on my stomach. I had a huge peanut stuck in my mouth. Yeah, we got to do the mouth to mouth, how sweet it was.

Rocky's first response when he noticed that there were no peanuts on the step or the landing was to look around. Turning in a complete circle, he was now looking directly at me and noticed the peanut in my mouth.

Rocky sat up and crossed his arms and contemplated the situation. He cocked his head to the side as if to confirm his decision; he brushed and smoothed out his fur. This was official. Rocky came down on all fours and sauntered over to me. He pressed his face to mine. We were nose to nose, eyeballing each other, then he sniffed me.

He sniffed my nose, my face, and even my ears. Then he moved around to my back and put his front foot and head on my back as if praying over me, blessing me, or both.

Then Rocky walked back around to face me. Facing me, he sniffed the peanut.

As Rocky sniffed the peanut, I could hear a little gurgling in his throat. Rocky licked his lips, opened his mouth, and bit down on the peanut. You could hear a little snap but no crack! He didn't pop the nut. He gently tugged as the peanut pulled out of my mouth, mission accomplished, peanut retrieved, the bonding was complete. Rocky turned around and ran down the steps into the yard, disappearing behind a bush.

I was excited with what just happened. I couldn't wait for Sue and Toren to get home. Sue just arrived, and as she was coming up the steps, I saw that she had some materials on losing weight. She was doing this Weight Watchers thing. Yeah, watching her weight go up! If she just kept watching her weight, she'd know why weight broke the bridge. I better shut up before I get in trouble. Sue had her big cherubic, childlike impish smile on her face. I kissed her.

I told her about Rocky and how he took the peanut out of my mouth. She couldn't stop laughing. She didn't believe me, but she knew it was probably true, knowing me too well.

With no prompting and perfect timing, Rocky flew down near us. He sat up and stared at Sue on cue. Sue had that kid's first Christmas look of amazement on her face. I immediately ran and got a peanut. I stuck it in my mouth and plopped down on the floor with the peanut sticking out of my mouth. And Rocky, the top-billing performer, took the peanut out of my mouth.

Sue was ecstatic. She was totally thrilled by Rocky. She asked, "Will Rocky do it for me?"

I kind of shrugged my shoulders and scratched my head. I looked at Rocky to see his reaction.

Rocky, sitting up on his hind legs, had his arms out like, "Cool, I don't care whom I get a peanut from. Ain't nut'n' but a nut! Crack 'em! Crack 'em!"

I told Sue he was ready to play "take the peanut out of my mouth" game. Sue got down on the floor and had the peanut sticking out of her mouth. And Rocky, like a real showbiz trooper, took the peanut out of Sue's mouth.

We all applauded and cracked up. I meant that seriously. Rocky was laughing and holding his stomach. Rocky was definitely part of the family.

It was hard to believe that with all this fun it would soon mark the beginning of paradise's end.

Elmo was observing carefully. He was not okay with this new family grouping.

That evening, as Toren returned, Sue and I shared our story about Rocky and how he was adopted into the family.

The following day started out in the usual way. Sue and Toren left for their work and school respectively.

The only change was that Elmo was down at the gate. Elmo acknowledged Sue and Toren with a good morning meow, but no one could touch Elmo at that point. After Sue and Toren had driven off, Elmo didn't run up the steps and slap me a paw-five as usual; he just looked at me as if he was saying, "Yeah, brotha! Oh yeah! This is the way it's gonna be."

Then Elmo flipped his tail up real high and straight. I think Elmo was trying to tell me something as he sauntered back across the street where he lived.

Nevertheless, I went back into the apartment. And no sooner had I closed the security door than I heard this loud thud against the security door. *Bam!*

Bam! There it was again! I whipped open the security door. And as I was looking around, I didn't see anyone or anything.

Then something hit me on the head. I grabbed my head as I looked up at the sunny blue California sky. Almost in silhouette, I could see Rocky coming down a branch that hung over our porch onto the roof. Rocky came down and perched on his hind legs and held his arms out with his hands stretched. I said to myself, "Wow, Rocky has hands!" I had never noticed that squirrels had hands, but then again, I've never been this intimately involved with a squirrel.

Anyway, Rocky had hands. I guess he was trying to gesture that he wanted a peanut.

Once again, Elmo was checking us out, taking notes at first and trying to stay cool and aloof like the great cats. He stayed cool when he would see Rocky taking peanuts from my mouth.

At the onset, I didn't really tune into what was happening, but Rocky had the natural instincts of a predator. I was beginning to feel like Dr. Doolittle, like a naïve numbskull, because I never thought of Elmo as a predator. Hey, we were family.

I had no idea foul play was at hand although the way the birds were chirping tweety and screaming kind of like, "Watch out, Rocky!" I should have known something was up. Then just out of the corner of my eye, I caught a glimpse of movement ever so slightly, so slowly—it was Elmo.

Elmo was moving close to the ground. His body was hugging the ground, as if preconditioning his muscles to be ready to spring and pounce at any given time as the opportunity presented itself.

I knew it was serious when Rocky jumped up on my shoulder and snatched the peanut out of my mouth and leaped off my shoulder and went airborne.

As Rocky was soaring, Elmo was also about to soar. Elmo leaped and it appeared as if Elmo would overtake Rocky in the game.

Rocky simply adjusted the flap of skin that flying squirrels have that allows them to fly. Rocky straightened his arms 180 degrees. He lifted his head up and off he went, gone in a split second.

Elmo was still soaring, but now he was soaring at nothing. And this totally confused him. He was dumbfounded. Elmo's face now had a wildly confused expression. He had a pitiful look, a look that happens before whatever perils a cat is about to face, happens. For Elmo, this was a big California tree happening!

Elmo hit the tree, *bam*. He dropped six feet to the ground, *bam!* Elmo just lay there facedown, sprawled out and helpless.

Elmo finally got up. He sort of pulled himself together and then staggered across the street heading home.

It was now obvious that Elmo was trying to get Rocky. Elmo was trying to surprise attack Rocky by jumping out of the bushes from behind trees. Elmo even tried to get up in Rocky's tree.

Rocky was starting to get a little annoyed with all this harassment. Elmo was waging mostly a ground war. Rocky began to retaliate with an air attack. Rocky started flying through the air, hitting Elmo with rocks and pebbles. Sometimes Rocky would just throw a handful of dirt at Elmo.

I attempted to reason with Elmo. "Rocky's dropping stuff on you. Rocky has hands and they can hold things like a brick. If Rocky got a running start down that long branch, he could hit the roof for added momentum, ricochet off the roof, and fly through the air with high velocity and air speed, then throw that brick and hit your butt. What are you going to do? You'll end up scratching on my door with your head wrapped, asking for aspirin. You better give Rocky some respect. Can't we all get along? This is L.A., Elmo! Hey, are you listening, Elmo? You should try to be friends with Rocky, you won't outsmart him, you ain't quick enough. The bottom line is that Rocky can kick your butt, so just chill."

It got bad. Rocky even added a ground attack. Rocky started chasing and running Elmo out of the yard, and Elmo would run and retreat to his camp. He would regroup and then return. Elmo was stubborn and he was not a quitter, just a poor loser and a bad sport.

One day, as I was driving up the street, I saw what appeared to be a fur stole on the ground. I parked the car and began walking toward the apartment. My attention was still on the fur piece. The closer I got to the fur piece, the more it began to look like a small animal. I bent over and picked up a stick. Taking the stick, I turned the fur over and screamed—it was Rocky.

Rocky was stretched and smashed, flatter than a cartoon. I ran back to the car and got a paper bag out of the trunk. Running back to Rocky, I took the stick and started to lift Rocky into the bag so that the family and I could give Rocky a proper sendoff.

As I was getting Rocky's body into the bag, Elmo came sauntering over, slinking out from one of the big California trees in the yard. Elmo's body language exuded a lot of pride. Elmo seemed to take exceedingly great pride in rubbing up, down and around the tree, his back humping while wiggling his tail. He then meowed. He did everything but beat his chest like Tarzan.

Elmo began walking arrogantly toward me; his face had a smug look. He had a "cat who swallowed the canary" look.

I was starting to get just a little disgusted and fed up with this attitude. I yelled at Elmo, "Did you do this, Elmo? Answer me!"

Elmo slithered through the wrought-iron gated fencing around the yard. And right at the edge of the grass, the part that extends a half a foot, give or take, outside the fencing, Elmo stopped and bent down.

I couldn't see what Elmo was doing, although I could hear him make a slight snapping sound with his mouth!

As Elmo raised his head up, I saw what made the snapping sound. I screamed, "My god! You pushed Rocky in front of a car, didn't you? You took the peanut out of his mouth! All I got to say to that is that you're a cold cat, Elmo!"

COOL CAT

The Cool Cat—that's what I called this very sophisticated, self-assured lady. Very cool was this cat.

Yeah, Cool Cat was a lady—a classy, sassy, confident, midnight black beauty.

Her hair was silky smooth, shiny, and so black. She was a black beauty, and she knew it, just a matter of fact, not bragging.

It was as if through her intelligence and the knowing of this, gave her an insight into her spirit and purpose in life. Cool Cat knew who she was—a cool customer. A real Cool Cat, an authority figure of equal priority to life, just the way God designed it! God does not play favorites. God is about order, not rank and file, have and have-not, and whether man or woman is superior.

Cool Cat knew better. She was into the natural laws. Cool Cat lived by the natural laws of God; she instinctively knew them. She had a special character and loved everyone equally.

And Cool Cat was born with this intuition. Cool Cat was a lot like my mother. If Cool Cat could have been a human, she would have been the Fifth Element, the missing link, the perfect woman.

Ah, that's a revelation, the universal problem that there are very few perfect women, which would distort motherhood, the fall from grace. And that left men needing to drink or take the Fifth and then freak out at Central Park.

But Cool Cat, like my mother, was the Fifth Element; perhaps that's why I took her into my confidence. She was perfect, like my wife. Cool Cat was a blessing. These are the natural laws of God's love. I call it all joy.

Before I run off in another direction, I will begin with my introduction to Cool Cat.

I walked up the walkway to my apartment one day, and from out of nowhere, this cat sauntered gracefully toward me. She walked as if she was on a mission.

As the cat on a mission approached me, it reminded me of how I was once stalked by Fast Fannie, a hungry adversary, a fallen woman, a she-devil, a man-eater in human form, a mutant worse than Dracula. Beware of fallen women, they got balls, they ain't a kitty cat.

This didn't seem to be the present situation as the cat came nearer. I could see a softness in its green compassionate eyes, full of love, gentle and humane.

The cat's eyes were nothing like Fast Fannie's. Fannie's eyes had a lustful fire of passion and conquest filled with carnivorous, primal instinct.

Without realizing it, I had come to a complete stop, just standing there, almost in a hypnotic state of euphoria.

I was standing there thinking to myself, God really did create a utopia, but man just doesn't know how to live in it because man puts his faith in dead presidents instead of the living God.

This was a feeling, and a glow of a recharged appreciation of just being alive, to be in the moment. And in this moment, the cat was gently rubbing and pressing on my legs. The cat was purring, and the purring had a melodious sound, sweet, gentle, with rhythmic and soothing tones.

The tones had a calming effect on me. The kind of effect that is similar to a mother humming to a child. It's that peaceful, serene hum of a Fifth Element mother.

It's that Fifth Element that gives a child the feeling that everything, is right with all of life and only good prevails, no matter how messed up the circumstances were. Keep the faith, keep the law of love, and hope will stay alive!

Okay, wake up, Dorothy. Break out of the euphoric utopianism, you're back in Kansas, and on your way back to Compton, California. I laughed out loud as I bent down and began stroking the cat.

I actually wasn't stroking the cat; it was more like I was holding my hand in the right position and the cat was massaging and comforting itself, for the cat knew all of its comfort spots.

I remember saying to the cat, "Aren't you the grand one!"

And no sooner had the words been spoken than the cat just fell to the ground on its back and opened itself up to me! I began to rub the cat's underside gently and respectfully. It purred and pawed at my hand, never once exposing or using a claw.

I said, "Aw, this cat is so cool."

And bing! That's it—"Cool Cat." That would be its name, but I asked first, "How do you like the name 'Cool Cat?' Is that cool with you?"

The cat rolled and flipped around with a suggested delight. So I guess the name "Cool Cat" was cool!

In the early stages of our relationship, it felt more like a courtship now that I think about it. Cool Cat would always and mysteriously appear from different areas of the yard. Cool Cat would almost always have some little romantic gift, something to share with me! One time it was a flower, another time it was a mouse.

Sometimes Cool Cat would just watch me feed the birds. The fascinating part was that Cool Cat never chased or attacked the birds, even when they sat on my shoulders. Cool Cat would simply lie at my feet.

And when I picked flowers for the apartment, Cool Cat would follow me around, as if to approve.

Even though I did most of the talking, Cool Cat seemed to understand everything I said.

It got so that Cool Cat began to recognize my friends, especially Darryl Dane Bohanan, a.k.a. DDB, who would always remark, "For somebody who's not pro cats, cats seem to be pro you!"

For the most part, I had never really given Cool Cat's gender any real thought. I never viewed Cool Cat as a male or female; it was just Cool Cat.

Nevertheless, it would take a dear friend and brother of mine, Gary Baker, to be the one to bring Cool Cat's positive gender identity (PGI) out of the closet, so to speak.

Gary arrived one bright sunny afternoon. Cool Cat and I had just gathered in the yard for a little picnic and splendor in the grass.

Gary walked over to us and shook his head and started pointing one of his well-manicured fingers and began reading us. "If this hussy ain't got her nerve. If this hussy was a woman, I'd call your wife and bust you."

I was slightly flabbergasted; where did he get this hussy read from? I was stammering somewhat as I inquired, "Gary, what are you saying?"

Gary blew out a mouthful of air and began to break down the facts of life. It was like Anatomy 101, "For the Reality of Deprived Mick E.", Gary began the lecture.

"Mick E., this is a real pussycat!"

As Gary was breaking the Fine Art of Reality to me, Cool Cat had cuddled up to Gary and was pressing and rubbing against Gary, almost star-struck.

As Gary's hand was following the contour of Cool Cat's humping back with his well-manicured index finger like a magician, Gary caught the swirl of Cool Cat's tail.

With a subtle tug, Gary yanked Cool Cat's tail straight up and proclaimed, "Oh, this is a real pussycat. See, no nuts here, pussy."

I tried to play this whole scene down. I was a little defensive. I blurted out, "Gary, she's a lady!"

Gary rolled his eyes upward. This day Gary was dressed GQ casual with a white sleeveless T-shirt, belted tailored slacks, and some penny loafers, a no-socks look!

Gary's hair and mustache were styled like Clark Gable's, without a hair out of place. Even as he ran his hand along the side of his head, the hair was laid, and Gary began to deliberate on our conception of Cool Cat.

He began. "You defend a cat because I refer to her as a hussy. Yet I call your wife Ma Frickett and you fall on the floor laughing. I call this hussy Da Real Pussy and you defend her like she was your mama or your wife! You need to take a nap while I call your wife and tell her about this pussycat."

I looked at Cool Cat. Cool Cat looked at me, and we both looked at Gary and we fell laughing, rolling and frolicking in the splendor of the grass.

We settled down, Gary lying on his stomach. I was on my back, and Cool Cat was between us, on her side, resting with her head on my shoulder.

After the laughter had died down and we had gotten very mellow, I asked Gary, "How did the Gay Rights Walk-A-Thon go?"

Gary replied, "I'm pooped, Mother is tired. The walk was fine, but these boots weren't made for walking.

I was cracking up at the sincerity and dry matter-of-factness of Gary's delivery. Then I gave him the pop quiz. "Gary, what would you do if they had a Gay Run-A-Thon next week?"

Gary said, "Them hags will have to handle it on their own. I may be white and a sissy, but I ain't crazy. If you see me running, it will be after a man, okay?"

I'm thinking, Miss Cool Cat, it really didn't make a difference to me. Whatever, I was not dealing with gender, sex, human or animal. I was dealing with the spirit of love. Me and Cool Cat was in love.

It's all about love. Love one another, love your despicable neighbor who probably is your public enemy. Still got to love your enemy. With God, it's all about love. It's the spirit of salvation. This miserable world that seems to be going to hell in a hand basket was saved for Christ's sake.

That's powerful, that's a lot of love, God's will. Through the law and through Cool Cat, I was being shown love. The force is with me!

In our love, I only made one mistake with my darling Cool Cat, Lady Cool.

Yeah, you guessed it. I fed her—a big mistake! I took an independent, confident, sole survivor and turned her into a welfare case: spoiled, screaming, demanding, and dependent.

Cool Cat would come around begging for handouts at 1:00 or 2:00 a.m. and my neighbors would begin to complain.

I discovered that there were unwritten cat laws. If you feed a cat, you have to take it in or move. I tried to be rational and calm with Cool Cat. At first I said, "No more food." What I hadn't come to, was the realization that what I was asking was like trying to get a junky to go cold turkey.

We had our first lovers' spat, and if Cool Cat would have been a woman, domestic violence would have been the scenario.

Cool Cat came a-yellin' and wailin', and it was at that moment that I fully understood why in all the movies and cartoons, people were always throwing stuff and shooting at cats. It isn't right, but I understand. The principle to domestic violence is that it ain't right, but I understand.

In fact, I was about to be one of those people myself because when I jumped out of my bed, I had murder on my mind. I was talking to myself, heading for the door.

I snatched the door open, and the first thing Cool Cat did was to try and run into the apartment. I blocked her with my foot and pushed her back into the hall.

She yelped as if I really kicked her, then she started that arrogant welfare cry.

Meanwhile, some neighbor was yelling down from upstairs, "Take that damn cat in or move out!"

I reached down and grabbed Cool Cat by the scuff of her neck and opened the security door and flung her out into the night and closed the door.

She stood there in shock. Her mouth was making meowing gestures, yet there was no sound.

It was obvious she was devastated, speechless. However, her eyes said it all. She was hurt and deeply wounded. She then turned and blended in with the darkness of the yard and vanished into the night.

I didn't see Cool for several days. I'll have to admit I was lonely. I had friends and associates, but Cool Cat was real company. We shared an open relationship with a higher spiritual awareness.

Time passed and I pushed the desire to see Cool Cat back in my mental files, psychologically on pause. I had put her on hold.

Whenever I would go out to the store, the gym, or whatever, I would always anticipate seeing Cool Cat while at the same time I tried to deceive myself I wasn't even thinking or making a conscious effort to hold any thoughts of Cool Cat. Remember, I had those thoughts on hold.

I guess some things truly are destined and others are just accidents which are unexplainable, due to the lack of understanding of the natural laws of cause and effect and the ripple effect of trying to know too much.

I know this much. I made some serious miscalculations with my relationship with Cool Cat; just as I did with my wife, and my wife is a lot like Cool Cat. I have made serious mistakes with my wife; nevertheless, she's still with me. So I'll handle Cool Cat like I handle my wife—keep the faith and trust her, and get out of the way. And before I could formulate another spiritual axiom, there she was.

I opened the outer gate, and there she was. She was lying stately and elegantly royal, her divine coolness herself, Cool Cat.

I stood in the doorway and felt like Rhett Butler of *Gone with the Wind*. Standing there looking gallantly at Scarlet. Only in this modern version Rhett gives a damn!

I didn't exactly rush to Cool Cat, but with great expediency I was up the four steps to the landing as she lay in front of my apartment door.

I crouched down, and Cool Cat leaped up on me. She had her front legs wrapped around my neck. She was hugging me and purring like a lawn mower. She was happy, but I truly believe I was happier.

I was so delirious and drunken with joy that I didn't even realize I had opened the apartment door. And like a bride and groom, we crossed the threshold. Cool Cat was like an ecstatic new bride in a honeymoon suite.

She jumped from my arms and began frantically running! She kept running through the apartment like she was trying to find something. I stood there in the middle of the living room. Standing there, I watched her dash into the kitchen like a bullet. She then shot out of the kitchen and zipped under the dining room table, straight into the hallway, between the living room, bathroom, and my bedroom.

Coming out of the bathroom, she darted into the bedroom out of my sight.

As I walked into the hallway from the living room, I entered the bedroom and there was Cool Cat, sitting on the middle of the bed.

I started laughing. I said, "I don't know what movies you been watching lately. Well, let me set the record straight. I found you, fed you, but you can get out of my bed, it ain't that kind of party. The only woman who gets in that bed with me is Mrs. Jones."

Cool Cat was in the house, but she was not staying in the house. She had visiting rights only, to be used at her own discretion between the hours of eight o'clock in the morning to ten forty-five in the evening, and Cool Cat had impeccable timing.

One of the things Cool enjoyed in the apartment was looking at the family pictures on display. Although she loved looking at the other various framed pictures and treasured works of some very gifted and talented people who had shared their inner spiritual projected expressions with me.

It was the show and tell of the stories that went with the family pictures.

Cool Cat was into family pictures. Cool Cat was into family.

As I picked Cool Cat up in my arms, we approached a picture of Amy and me. I told Cool, "See this picture here? It's the day Amy, my niece, married me. So that makes you my third wife. Amy is very bold, like you! And a sophisticated lady, just like you, but not as humble and wise. Amy was five years old when she proposed marriage to me. We were on a beach in Boston or Connecticut. I don't remember, I just knew I now had two wives, Sue and Amy. And sooner or later you clash with your wives, and I've been clashing with Amy, especially now that she's grown up and has another husband, Duncan. I don't know what he's about, I just know that Amy and I are clashing. She thinks I'm cynical, but I think I'm a realist. I think she's an idealist, you know, the rose-colored glasses syndrome. Amy thinks I think life is black-and-white. She feels life is shades of gray."

I muddled this "shades of gray" concept over in my mind. Then I thought that if life is shaded gray, then why is all of the so-called important stuff documented on white paper and the important information in black?

This was when I was introduced to the law of Amy. And this law was that if Amy can't win, you must agree not to disagree with Amy. Amy was clever.

Many months had passed and Cool Cat seemed to have become inaccessible. Then one day, there came a scratching and a meowing at the door. As soon as I opened the door, she darted into the apartment and ran into the hall closet next to the bathroom.

Once she was in the closet, she started moving things around as if to make room for something.

I was curious, so I just yelled out, "Hey, Cool, what's up? What's with all this rearranging the closet?"

Cool had come to a halt, and she started walking to me with this look in her eyes that I could not recognize. Even the way she rubbed up on me was different. When I picked her up, she was heavier and quite fat. It hit me. I screamed, "You're pregnant and you're about to deliver!"

As soon as the realization of the expectancy set in, I went from husband and friend to an irate father. I was in shock. "Oh no, you ain't pregnant! And you think I'm gonna let you turn this closet into an emergency room? I made a big mistake feeding you, but I won't be that big a fool and let you drop your kitty litters here, oh no! No! No, you won't have my neighbor tar and feather me and run me out of my home! I don't think so, not here in this house."

Holding Cool Cat in my arms, we were now face to face, facing another adversity in our relationship. Looking into each other's eyes intensely, probing each other in depth, we kept our silence, each in our own thoughts, trying to figure out what must be done.

Cool Cat's eyes expressed it all—forgiveness and understanding. She purred and nuzzled me. She then indicated she wanted to get down and get busy; she instinctively knew what she had to do. I placed her gently down, and she scurried out of the hallway and through the living room and waited by the door. Waiting for me to let her go.

I opened the door, and she went out! I closed the door and I wept. Time, which waits on no one, had passed so quickly; and it is so with true love—absence makes the heart grow fonder.

The more I thought about Cool Cat, the fonder my memories of Cool Cat had become, and the deeper the appreciation of the aesthetics and uniqueness of our love which had manifested over time. The true value of God's existence in heaven and on earth in things we experience and do if we believe that God exists in all things.

I had to find her. I opened the door, and there she was, as cool as ever. I could see in Cool's eyes that she was glad to see me. I picked her up, and she immediately threw her forelegs around my neck. True love is sweet.

She was purring like a new motor. And I was laughing, rubbing, and caressing her. I was rekindling the old flame. I noticed that Cool Cat wasn't fat any longer. She was slender and a black beauty again. I shouted, "Where are the babies?"

Cool Cat wiggled down and slid under a space at the bottom of the security door and disappeared to the left of the building under a bush.

I could hear Cool. She was meowing, and it actually sounded like baby talk or the way a mother talks to a baby.

There were five babies, and Cool was gently nudging them, teaching them. She slid under the door. As she came up on the inside of the door, she encouraged them to do the same, and they did.

Cool Cat came over to me. The babies watched her every move, watching as she rubbed up against me, purring and rolling over on her back. I rubbed her and talked in a low, soft tone of love.

As Cool Cat and I shared our bond, the babies came over. They began rubbing up against me, touching me with their little paws and playfully teething on my fingers.

We all sat gathered on the concrete floor at the bottom of the steps that led to my apartment.

I began to name the kitties according to their coloring characteristics. I started with Tip, who was all black except for the tip of its tail, and so this was Tip. Next was Foot. Foot had all its blackness with the exception of one white foot. Patch was white, except for a patch of black around its left eye. Then there was Star, whose totally white face stood out from its smooth black body, like a shining star in a black sky. Finally there was Fluffy, a little fluffy ball of hair. It had the marking of the others—a white face with a black patch on the ear, one white foot, and a white tip on the top part of its fluffy tail.

Cool Cat came by daily with the family. And one day, trailing to the rear of Cool and her babies was a big white cat. The kitties were so well behaved, and they sat at my feet peacefully. Cool was doing a tremendous job, and she was a Fifth Element mother, a credit to womanhood.

Cool Cat, ever so gracious and thoughtful, had begun to rub up on me. I knelt down on my knees, and we were face-to-face and we rubbed noses. She seemed to wink her eyes at me. Then she turned toward the big white cat, as if to summon it over.

At this moment, it appeared that all eyes were focused on the big cat, which stood statuesque. In this stillness, the cat glowed as the sunlight reflected and illuminated off it like a celestial light.

It was breathtakingly hypnotic and then the trance was broken by the commanding attention of the big cat's majestic and powerful movement toward me.

As the cat came within touching distance of me, it stood up, as if to shake hands.

I stuck both of my hands out, palms up. The cat's front two paws fell gently into my hands, and I pulled the cat toward me.

After getting a good hug, the cat got down and rolled on the grass, much in the same manner as Cool Cat had done on our first meeting.

I rubbed the cat's underside, and with great amazement, I excitedly said, "You got balls. Congratulations, Papa! Let's go see the family. I'm going to call you Whitey."

Everybody followed me into the apartment. I was like the cat pied piper.

Once in the apartment, I got everybody comfortable, but I told them immediately that I wasn't feeding them but I would give them water. I papered the floor just in case.

I started showing them pictures on one of my walls and got around to Sue's photograph. "This is Sue, my wife, the greatest gift God has given me. And God has given me many gifts, and you're a witness of this yourself, a gift to me. Ironically we're similar to you two cats. Sue's white and I'm black. You guys are black and white and you're still cats, but with humans, black and white is a social conflict of division and separation of the human race. Isn't that sad about humans? This is the gray area my niece Amy is always referring to."

I had a profound impact on the cats as they gathered around me, almost as if to sympathize and comfort me and support our family. I felt blessed. Then again, I guess no matter how good it seems to be, there is always eventually the downside of life. Even Christ had to experience that in the end, hanging on the cross. It's like you always know when the end is coming; it's like the quiet before the storm.

Parting can be such a sweet sorrow, and that sorrow would come in a subtle way. In my mind, we had all become one family and time would define this for me.

One day, as I was coming out of the apartment, Whitey was standing at the edge of the walkway crying. He had a whine, like someone singing the blues. I walked up softly behind Whitey and bent over and rubbed his back. He humped up, and he was very tense. I could feel the stress.

I looked at Whitey looking up the street and I saw why he was singing the blues. Cool Cat was being cat-napped by some lady and taken away in a car; she was already in a cage. Cool Cat saw us and she cried out. We heard her even though the car's windows were up. We knew this was a goodbye. And as much as Whitey and I wanted to do something, there was nothing we could do. It was devastating to us, and we had to accept the change. As Cool Cat looked deep into my eyes, I could tell she heard my heart-filled thoughts. I could see the tears in her eyes. I was crying, and then the car drove away.

Two of the kitties, Star and Foot, were taken in by a neighbor. Tip was dead; a neighborhood dog attacked him. I never knew what happened to Fluffy and Patch; they just disappeared one day.

With the tides of life shifting, all Whitey could do was cry the blues. All I could do was use the power of my mind and speak telepathically to Cool Cat a simple thought. "Thank you, Cool Cat, my fair lady, for you have been the fairest of them all. Thank you, my sweet darling, and I can't even say goodbye."

I looked down, and Whitey was gone too. I was alone.

JOJO: THE CAT FROM HELL

It's amusing in a suspicious, perplexing, elliptically obscured sort of way, the way in which our society worldwide can use words to represent or misrepresent people, places, and things.

Take the word *black*, for instance. *Black* has been used to symbolize evil and the art of black magic. On the other hand, take the word *white*; it has been used to symbolize pureness and the angelic realm. Basically, white is good and mostly the symbol for who's in charge.

Black and *white* are just words; yet they represent colors, word coloring, or the colors of words, as well as the hidden content of social codes. It's the divide-and-conquer culture of worshiping your own bullshit.

This culture of self-proclaimed spiritual superiority has become contagious. It has penetrated into our spiritual DNA and is affecting our mental state and creating identity loss and mental blackouts. Black is the color most depicted negatively. Witches wear black, especially evil witches. And these witches always have a black cat to go with their black magic. Why? Who Knows? Ask Magic Johnson.

The peculiarity of all of this witch blackness is that the person is always white. I guess this is the gray area my niece Amy always refers to. She has to rethink everything because she sees my viewpoint of life as being black-and-white. Actually the reverse is true. Nevertheless, my niece could be 100 percent right.

At one point, I had spoken with this world-famous astrologer, Lillian Bono. She told me, "Your faith will be challenged and tried. You will have an opportunity to renew and strengthen your faith."

I asked her why my faith was going to have to go through such a transformation.

She predicted, "A black cat is going to cross your path and this will be a cat from hell."

I was sipping a glass of wine and thinking out loud. "A black cat from hell is going to cross my path. Hmmm, that's like saying Satan's coming to visit me in the form of a black cat."

Without so much as letting my thoughts continue, Lillian interjected, "No, not Satan, but close."

I almost choked. I started shaking my head. Was this the spiritual ritual of the chosen? So I asked, "What is it with this cat from hell? What the hell am I going to do with a cat from hell?"

She started laughing hysterically, fell out of her chair, and was rolling around the carpeted floor. She inhaled and then went into a meditative mode with her eyes closed. Holding her ring-clustered hand to her head, she spoke with a trancelike voice with a power that flowed through her words like the Nile. Like scripture, her stream of consciousness reverberated in my ear as she revealed the prophecy. She spoke by divine will.

She continued. "I'll tell you what you're supposed to do. You'll do the will of the Divine One, the one who has aligned the planets for you. Do what you do best, love. Love the hell out of the cat from hell. That's all, goodbye."

Goodbye. So she was reading my past, present, and future. Wow. Hel-lo!

Quite a bit of time had passed, and I had forgotten about the cat from hell until my wife's friend Peggy came over. It all started one evening when Peggy began banging on our living room window. She was banging on the window frantically, with this glazed-over look in her eyes as if she had seen something or had experienced something soul-stirring.

As I turned to go to the door, I got a glimpse of Peggy clutching something. I opened the door for her. I had barely cracked the door open when Peggy bolted past me. She had that look people have in scary movies. In fact, Peggy looked like someone from those old black-and-white horror movies.

You know, the ones where the woman sees the invisible man taking off his bandages and he unravels to nothing. And that's the part in the movie when the witches start to scream. That's what Peggy looked like to me at that moment.

She threw the mysterious object she was clutching onto the hardwood floor. It made a nasty sound.

Sue and I were standing there, staring at Peggy, staring at the object, which turned out to be a black cat in a cage. I threw my hand to my head, with my eyes shut. I clinched my teeth and thought to myself, "Oh no, the cat from hell, it can't be!" I kept repeating that over and over in my mind.

And suddenly, I'm hearing Peggy ranting and raving, "Please take him, I need a break, I need a rest, I need a Valium!"

Then she turned and bolted out the door, running to her car, saying, "JoJo, JoJo, God help them!" Then she drove off. She put the pedal to the metal, with gravel and dirt kicking up. Her car raised a cloud of dust as she sped away.

I walked over and closed the door. As I turned around, I could see Sue had already started to get involved with the cat. She had it out of the cage. She was talking the way women talk to kids—you know, that phony mama voice.

I felt like a person who was caught in a twister and had survived, then got caught up in another one. This was how I felt as I tried to get Sue to help me put this into focus and proper perspective. I spoke up. "Sue darling, what's going on here? Why is this cat here?"

Sue simply smiled and said, "It's a nice cat, huh?"

I was scratching my head and rubbing my mouth. I felt that I had been violated. I was a little upset with the situation, and I related that to Sue. "Sweetheart, we don't own a cat. We never bought a cat. I also don't remember either of us saying that we need or want a cat, then why is a cat here?"

All she said was, "Mick E., the cat is here because Peggy left it here. So here it is! A nice cat, huh?"

I was starting to hold my breath so as not to scream. I exhaled to feel calmer. As I began to speak, I could hear the edge in my voice. "Sue, Peggy left here like a person from a scary movie and I'm sure it had something to do with that cat."

Sue said, "Well, let me explain. It's obvious that Peggy is having some problems."

So I replied, "Sue, the problem is this. Peggy has a problem with the cat and she dropped the problem here. I have a problem with that."

She said, "Honey, you shouldn't have a problem with anything. You always said we are problem solvers. He really doesn't seem to be a problem."

I needed strength at this point. So I said, "Peggy ran away screaming 'JoJo, JoJo, help them.' That sounds like a problem. This cat JoJo has got to go, he sounds like a problem."

And when the cat heard its name, it got off Sue's lap and came over and rubbed up on me. I admit I was affected. I softened my position. So I said, "Okay, he doesn't seem to be a problem. He's got the luck of the Irish, I know that. I wonder if Ireland has any black Irish, I know there are black Jews."

So I went to the neighborhood pet store to get supplies. JoJo had it going on. JoJo was in the house and seemed normal, but this was the weekend. The real JoJo would appear as soon as Sue left for work on Monday morning.

After Sue left for work, I was left with JoJo, his true personality was still incognito, still normal.

Being an entertainer and trying to keep up with the business, I was going to take a tap lesson and off I went. I came back, and as I entered the apartment, I saw JoJo chilling, but his eyes had the expression of a villain, a scoundrel.

I started feeling a *"Wile E. Coyote"* vibe in the apartment. I walked through the living room, bedroom, dining room and family room looking for signs of trouble. I was about to learn and get a clear understanding of JoJo's warped personality. As I headed into the kitchen, I saw broken plates and glasses on the floor. Pots and pans were scattered, and all the burners on the stove were on.

I screamed and turned around like a race driver coming out of a sharp turn avoiding a skid. I was walking fast, hard and steady.

As I went back into the family room, I confronted JoJo who had by now, climbed onto the windowsill, catching the last rays of a gorgeous sunset. He was draped on the windowsill, looking at me like I had a problem. Suddenly, I felt like the bad guy and then I turned and went back to the kitchen and cleaned up the mess.

I got dinner ready, then went and sat on my bed, and that was when I noticed sooty paw prints going up the wall right to the ceiling. The paw prints went halfway up to the middle of the ceiling and then they stopped.

As I bent backward looking over my head, I could see footprints going down the opposite wall—right to the top of our pillows!

I heard a sound of something running very fast. While I had been doing a little light analytic deducing, I was coming to the conclusion that these were the sooty paw prints of JoJo. As I realized this, JoJo had gotten off the windowsill and was down on the floor, running like he was in an Olympic event and going for the gold.

I couldn't believe what I was seeing. JoJo was scaling the bedroom walls right up to the middle of the ceiling, then dropping down onto the bed. He jumped off the bed and hit the floor with such a force that it propelled him forward. He increased his speed and then repeated the same maneuver backwards!

It's true, these were not high ceilings, but it was like being inside of a twister. I was amazed. As I began to ease off the bed and out of JoJo's swirling, twisted momentum, I went into the kitchen and got the broom.

Returning with broom in hand and holding it with both hands, I placed it at the path of JoJo's vortex. *Whap!* JoJo met the broom head-on. *Whap, whap!* He was hit.

JoJo lay there, eyes crossed, tongue hanging out of his mouth. He looked up at me like, "That was cool."

If Disney's Goofy was a drug addict, I believe he would have looked like JoJo did the time that he locked himself in the bathroom and raided the medicine cabinet.

I had just returned from an audition, and I was feeling real up. I entered the apartment, and I could see that JoJo had been circling the walls and ceiling, then I noticed that he had attacked the curtains and shades, a rip here, a rip there.

I started looking around the apartment for the broom. I suddenly heard a thumping noise; it was coming from behind the closed bathroom door.

As I walked toward the bathroom, the thumping noise got louder. I heard JoJo meowing and smashing stuff. I turned the doorknob, and it was locked. I couldn't believe it! JoJo had locked himself in the bathroom.

As I was screaming, I went to get the toolbox. I was really going to fix Mr. JoJo. I screwed off the doorknob, and after pushing the door open, I slowly glanced around the room. The medicine cabinet was open, and a lot of Sue's medication was knocked down. I noticed that the top was off of one of the bottles. When I bent down to pick up the scattered pills, I came face-to-face with JoJo.

JoJo's head and the top half of his body was hanging over the toilet. His front legs were extended with his paws gripping the edge of the seat. JoJo's lower body was down in the toilet, and I felt like flushing him down!

I would have flushed him, except that he looked comically goofy. He had inhaled some of the medicine. I pulled him out of the toilet and cleaned the bathroom. And one thing with JoJo, was that he never did the same mischievous thing more than once, at least never the same way.

One time I was taking a bath and JoJo ran into the bathroom and dove headfirst into the tub and started swimming. He did the dog paddle and swatted the soap.

JoJo kept us on our toes. He certainly kept me on guard, and he definitely had my attention. Nearly the last straw for JoJo was when I was sitting naked on the edge of the bed after a bath. I was quite relaxed and my mind was completely off JoJo, who was tunneling under the blanket, which was on the floor, half off the bed. He was barreling along leaving just enough space for a small child or sadistic cat to crawl through unnoticed.

Meanwhile, I was totally absorbed watching a sporting event on TV, and JoJo had tunneled his way through the covers and was heading toward my dangling testicles. The next thing I knew was that pain was shooting through my groin. I released a bloodcurdling scream! JoJo had smacked my testicles like a boxer hitting a punching bag.

I jumped up so high I almost hit my head on the ceiling. When I hit the floor, I took off running for the broom. JoJo took off running for his life.

I got the broom and was swinging it at JoJo with skill. If it wasn't for Sue walking in at that moment screaming, accompanied by my friend Gary, he would have died.

JoJo slowly eased out from behind the bookcase trying to look pitiful. As in the case with Cool Cat, Gary would witness another cat dilemma in my life. With raised eyebrows, he stuck one of his well-manicured fingers in the air, arching it downward toward JoJo and said; "And who is this pitiful-looking black sad sack?"

Wrapping a towel around myself, I began to give Gary some history on JoJo. Gary cracked up and found my cat perils very entertaining.

We went to the kitchen and I poured Gary a glass of champagne. While Gary was being entertained, JoJo had shifted personalities. He no longer looked pitiful and had taken on his nightmare stare.

JoJo was in stalking mode. He had been watching Gary's hands. Gary used his hands a lot. JoJo spied the champagne that I had served Gary, which was sitting on the floor in a long-stemmed green crystal glass.

Gary reached down to pick up his drink, and JoJo swatted his hand, scratching it and drawing blood.

Gary screamed and dropped the glass, which smashed as soon as it hit the floor! Champagne spilled everywhere, mixed with pieces of shattered crystal. The champagne began spreading across the waxed hardwood floor like a river overflowing its banks.

Gary moved with the quickness of a mongoose attacking a rattlesnake. Gary's hand snaked out like lightning, striking, grabbing JoJo by the throat and neck so that he couldn't bite or scratch him. And with his other hand, Gary picked up the Yellow Pages and was about to beat JoJo with it. Gary was screaming, "I'll show you what happens when you scratch Mother! They will find you in the paper under 'Deceased, Dead on Arrival'!"

It was in this dramatic moment that I understood what my astrologist truly meant. I could hear her words: "Mick E., you'll have to love the hell out of the cat from hell, love is what you do best."

Just as Gary was about to lower the boom, I ran to JoJo's defense, pleading, "No, Gary, no! Please don't hurt JoJo. I know he's a pain in the ass, but he needs love and to be loved like we all do. He needs affection, understanding, patience, forgiveness, and regeneration, please put him down."

Time came to a halt, and the room felt strangely silent. It was as if life had been put on pause, except for JoJo who looked up, looked at me, and then looked at Gary. He then began to shriek loud cries, like a neglected child's cry for acceptance. The spell had been broken.

Gary relaxed his grip on JoJo's throat. He slowly put down the phone book, and we all exhaled with relief together. Gary let JoJo drop gently to the floor. JoJo stood momentarily, as if recounting his entire life.

Then JoJo ran over to me. He began rubbing up on me, as if to thank me for caring so much for him. I picked up JoJo gently and hugged him. JoJo licked my face, and Gary wiped tears off his eyes.

The spell was over and love was on, with a mix of forgiveness, love, and happiness. Love will always drive hell out of a cat from hell.

MELVAN THE CAT

I discovered over time that domestic animals act a lot like the people they live with or associate with. And if that principle applies to animals, wouldn't it apply to children and people in general?

I came to that insightful conclusion only in hindsight. The environment—spiritual and physical—has a psychological influence on our emotions, both negative and positive. Raising children creates a psychological impact on them. The female psyche's spiritual trauma and the sins of the father are all recycled through your mama's drama. A dysfunctional adult with a short attention span is a reflection of this type of upbringing. And there goes the neighborhood!

People are indoctrinated by their parent's religious beliefs and ethnic prejudices. Politically correct, yet spiritually wrong, faking and inwardly shaking! What's all the faking and shaking about? It's scary! When you look to your inner environment, there's no substance, no strength, no love. Love helps us fight the good fight as children of God, so we fight for identity. Without a true spiritual identity, we are created and recreated by our own Antichrist.

For example, my oldest son is a former boxer like myself. His son Pepi likes to box as well. There's a common link between us. Pepi, who was only five years old at the time, would box with Melvan the cat. It turned out that Melvan was the real fighter, the boxing cat! Melvan was the cat's meow.

It was Melvan who proved to me without a shadow of a doubt that domestic animals are a lot like the people they live with. Once you recognize it in animals, seeing it in people's kids is scary. The environmental influence creates behavior patterns, not only genetics or DNA; it's the personal day-to-day contact.

My son, grandson, as well as myself, we all box. And now Melvan, linked by association, was a boxing cat. Melvan could box and fight. We're talking about throwing down, putting up, or shutting up!

Melvan would kick Garfield's butt, I'm serious. And Garfield ain't no slouch!

Melvan would whup Garfield like Macho Camacho beat Sugar Ray's butt; that was truly a butt whupin', A butt whipping from one ego to another big ego. Macho beat the little bit of sugar left out of Ray Leonard. It's the bittersweet of the pride that goes before the haughty fall from fame. Our egos always fall.

Melvan the cat didn't have a big ego like Sugar or Macho. Melvan walked by faith, not by ego, and Melvan had faith in his boxing, not his ego.

Melvan was cold when it came to boxing. He was a natural. He would watch the fights with us. Melvan loved to hear the announcer say, "Good evening, ladies and gentlemen, and bloodthirsty degenerate fight fans everywhere. We are ready to start this evening's barbaric event. Fighting out of the blue corner . . ."

And as the announcer would be saying this, Melvan would get up and go to a corner of the room. Melvan would start to warm up, shake his head, scratch behind his ear, stretch his front legs out, rub his paw across his nose, then blow his nose. He was just loosening' his shoulders up and would hunch his back a few times. He would drop down, then focus on the TV. Melvan was ready.

My son said, "Pops, Melvan looks like he wants to fight."

I replied, "He's got fighter instincts."

My son asked, "Pops, you really think Melvan can fight?"

I said, "Mess wit' him!"

My son started laughing. Then he called Melvan out. "Yo, Melvan, come here!"

Melvan looked at my son like Robert DeNiro did in *Taxi*. My son said, "Yeah, I'm talking to you, come here!"

Melvan calmly went over. He was very obedient and self-disciplined. As Melvan approached my son, the bell rang on the TV fight—*bing!*

My son said, "Okay, Melvan, let's get busy."

He took his index finger and started to finger jab three times at Melvan. Melvan ducked the first jab and parried the next two and shot a double left paw at my son. He then feinted a left paw at my son. As he jumped to his right, Melvan slapped my son with a right paw. *Pow!* Melvan meowed and I screamed, "Oops, upside yo head, oops upside yo head."

Then Melvan leapt up on my son's lap. Standing up, he jabbed my son in the nose. *Bop!* He whipped a right hook, *bop!*

My son, a second too late, pulled his left hand up, dropping his right hand, leaving his face wide open. Melvan looked at him dead straight in the eyes. That's the look when the opponent knows it's over. Melvan confidently flashed his left paw claw and meowed. I said, "Oops, there it is!"

My son screamed, "Hey, Melvan! I'm just joking, don't forget who's feeding you!"

After that reality check, we started to seriously train Melvan. We let him spar with my grandson Pepi. Melvan and Pepi boxing together was so cute. It was wonderful to watch a child like Pepi interact with Melvan, what a joy! It was family entertainment; there really is no place like home.

When Pepi and Melvan sparred, Melvan would mainly practice defense against Pepi. He let my grandson win most of the sessions. The cat would let my grandson chase him from room to room, and Pepi would brag, "I beat Melvan, I beat Melvan, I'm the greatest!"

But let my grandson mess with an electrical outlet, or try to sneak into the medicine cabinet, or play with harmful things like matches, and Melvan would fire him up and beat his butt! Pepi would scream, "Melvan's trippin'!"

Melvan's day of true atonement came when he had a box-off with Killah the dog. Killah was the neighborhood dog. I always used to joke that Killah held up a bank while singing, "Give up the kibbles and bits 'cause I'm kickin' butt."

Killah was not to be fooled with. This dog thought anything that messed with his dog food gave him a right to eat it or kill it. He did whichever came first.

On November 16, my son's birthday, we were having a party in my son's basement apartment. It was a wonderful celebration. As people were coming in and out of the apartment, Melvan escaped.

Time passed and nobody really missed or noticed Melvan's absence. Then again, when folks are partying, who notices anything?

Nevertheless, a guest who looked out the window suddenly shrieked, "Melvan!" No one seemed to hear or care until she said, "Oh my god . . . Killah."

The whole party came to a halt! This was a Kodak moment. We all rushed to the window. My son raised the window and screamed through the bars, "Come back, Melvan! Melvan, we love you, Melvan! Come back, Melvan, come back 'cause we ain't comin' out, we ain't about to deal with Killah! We can get another cat, but remember, we love you, Melvan!"

We all stood there, petrified with fear. Killah saw Melvan and growled his disdain, the "I'm the ruler" growl. Killah ran toward Melvan with the intent to take Melvan out. Meanwhile, we were all inside, cowardly screaming, "Run, Melvan, run! Run 'cause you are on your own, brother!"

Melvan just maintained his composure. Melvan was too cool. He didn't flinch. Melvan was iceberg-cat slim, just chillin'!

Unfortunately, Killah was not impressed. Killah broke on Melvan so quick that it was a blur—*wrrh, grrr, snap, growl!* Killah was trying to bite all nine lives out of Melvan at once.

Melvan was always too cool, the advanced thinker. Melvan went into a defensive posture. The cat sure had intestinal fortitude and he jumped out of the way with split-second timing—*whoosh!*

Melvan regrouped and hit Killah. *Bam, bam, bam!* Three left open-claw hooks. Razor hooks, baby! Cut!

Killah was surprised by the cut and was dazed. He ducked under another left hook, getting behind Melvan and quickly seeing a chance to get Melvan's testicles.

But before Killah could crack the power of the sacred cat nuts, the family jewels of Puss 'n' Boots, Melvan, the baddest boxing cat on Planet Earth, took action. With the quickness that was once Sugar Ray Robinson's, Muhammad Ali's, and Sugar Ray Leonard's, Melvan slid to his left, spun around, and threw an open claw right uppercut and came back with an open claw left hook cut.

Melvan was totally focused. He jabbed Killah in the nose and did a Jersey Joe Walcott pivot walk away then jumped up on a stack of boxes. Unfortunately, the boxes weren't stacked that high and were in a tight, narrow corner.

Killah growled as if to say, "Now whatcha gonna do, baby? Anywhere you think you can jump, I gotcha. It's Macho time, Sugar! Aarrrhh!" Killah was beside himself. Melvan quickly surmised his situation. Dropping down, he looked up. He checked Killah and looked up again. He recoiled as if to jump. Stretching his front legs upward, you could almost see him starting to ascend.

Killah sensed the jump with expectation. Killah jumped first. He put great effort in his thrust. Killah leapt with joy, rising with great expectations of catching Melvan in flight and ripping and tearing him from limb to limb.

As Killah was jumping, Melvan pulled back and dropped down as the dog soared up, up, up while Melvan calmly and coolly looked up and watched Killah sail over his head.

Melvan waited patiently as Killah's hind side passed overhead. Then he reached up and triple right-hooked Killah's family jewels, like a high-tech boxing speed bag.

Killah, let out a bloodcurdling howl of sheer agony. He'd been defeated and de-balled! The poor dog crashed into a wall and Melvan jumped on Killah's back, as if he were saying, "Take this, take that!"

Meanwhile, I'm screaming from my son's apartment, "Why must I always chase that cat! *Woof.* Must be da dawg 'n me! *Woof!*"

Or maybe it's just *Cat Tales: Da Real Pussy.*

Meow!

-THE END-

Made in the USA
Middletown, DE
24 May 2021